PEOPLES OF THE WORLD

ANDREW LANGLEY

The Bookwright Press
New York · 1986

Topics

The Age of the Dinosaurs
Castles
Earthquakes and Volcanoes
Great Disasters
Houses and Homes
Peoples of the World
Pollution and Conservation
Robots
Under the Ground

All the words that appear in **bold** are explained in the glossary on page 30.

First published in the
United States in 1986 by
The Bookwright Press
387 Park Avenue South
New York, NY 10016

First published in 1985 by
Wayland (Publishers) Ltd
49 Lansdowne Place, Hove
East Sussex BN3 1HF, England

ISBN 0-531-18059-X
Library of Congress Catalog Card Number: 85-73659

Phototypeset by Kalligraphics Ltd
Redhill, Surrey, England
Printed in Italy by
G. Canale & C.S.p.A., Turin

Contents

The Many Races of Mankind

Since our history began, people have moved widely over the earth. The first human beings probably lived in central Africa two million years ago. From there they spread northward to Europe and Asia, and as far as the Americas and Australia.

As they settled in different parts of the world, they adapted to the places where they lived. Those living

Australian aborigines' dark skin protects them from the sun.

People in colder climates have light skins.

near the hot **equator** had black skins, while those in the colder north had white skins. Some found fertile lands and became farmers, while others became hunters and fishermen.

Today there are more than 4,300 million people in the world, made up of hundreds of different races.

This farmer lives in Nigeria.

The "white" races live mainly in Europe and North America. The dark-skinned races live mainly in central and southern Africa, and those with yellow skins in China and the Far East. In South America and southern Asia there is a huge variety of peoples.

A Mongol woman making bread for her family.

We have not stopped moving around, and the races continue to mix and develop. Many Indians and Pakistanis now live in Britain. Europeans have settled in southern Africa. Jews from Poland and Germany have emigrated to North America.

This map will help you to find out where the peoples who are mentioned in the text live.

ARCTIC OCEAN
Norway
Great Britain
Ireland
Germany
Poland
France
Czechoslovakia
Spain
Italy
SIBERIA
U.S.S.R.
Mongolia
Japan
SAHARA DESERT
Saudi Arabia
Pakistan
China
PACIFIC OCEAN
India
Philippines
Sudan
S. Yemen
Yemen
Nigeria
Uganda
Somalia
Malaysia
Solomon Islands
Zaire
Kenya
Rwanda
Sumatra
New Guinea
Java
Bali
INDIAN OCEAN
Australia
South Africa

The Dark-skinned Peoples

The oldest human bones yet discovered were found in the Rift Valley in central Africa. They show that humans were living and hunting there nearly two million years ago. At that time ice covered a large part of the world. Only the area near the equator was warm enough for humans to survive.

When the **Ice Age** ended and the world grew warmer, the equatorial region became very hot indeed. So the people who lived there developed ways of protecting themselves from the heat. Their black skins kept out the harmful rays of the sun. Their wide noses helped to ventilate their bodies and cool them down quickly.

Africa is such a vast continent that there is a huge variety in the tribes that live there. The Watusi of

The tall Masai people of Kenya sleep in mud huts.

The Pygmy tribes of Zaïre live in the jungle.

Rwanda and the Masai of Kenya are the tallest peoples in the world. Many of them reach 2.1 meters (7 ft) in height. They are **nomads** and wander over a wide area to find grazing for their cattle. They sleep in mud huts at night, and herd the cattle into pens called kraals, to keep them safe from wild animals.

The shortest people in the world also live in Africa. These are the Pygmy tribes of Zaïre, who rarely grow taller than 1.5 meters (4 ft 9 in). This suits them perfectly for life in the jungle, where they can move quickly and quietly among the trees.

The Pygmies are nomads too. They roam the jungle, seeking food and shelter as they go. They catch antelope with nets woven from forest vines, and even kill elephants with their spears and arrows.

A Nigerian woman at the village well.

They climb the giant trees in search of fruit and wild honeycombs, and collect nuts and roots.

Today most Africans are farmers, or work in the big cities. The farmers face many problems. On the grasslands of countries such as Nigeria and the Sudan there is often not enough rain for the crops to grow. When the rain comes, it may be so hard that it causes flooding and washes away the topsoil. Every year, many thousands of people go hungry.

These people face other problems too. For many centuries the Zulus of southern Africa had grown grain on the coastal plains. But they were gradually driven out by the white Boer settlers, who took their lands. Today, many Zulus work as laborers on farms which now belong to white people.

There are rich deposits of precious minerals in South Africa. Gold and diamonds are mined from deep in the earth. Most of the laborers in these mines are black people, who have come from neighboring countries in search of work. They live in special compounds built by the mine owners.

Many centuries ago, black-skinned tribes spread across the Indian Ocean to the western Pacific. Their descendants can still be found today in the Philippines, New Guinea and the Solomon Islands.

Thousands of black Africans were forced to move to North America and the West Indies. They were captured or bought by slave traders, who shipped them across the Atlantic. There they were sold as slaves to work on cotton and sugar plantations. In 1863, slavery was ended in the United States. Today, 22 million black people live here.

Many black people in South Africa work in mines.

The Light-skinned Peoples

As people move farther from the equator, their bodies change to cope with the colder climate. Their hair grows more thickly to keep them warm. Their noses and lips are narrower. Their skin does not need so much protection from the sun, so it is pale. These people are known as **Caucasoids**.

Those with the whitest skins are the people of Scandinavia. Many are tall, with blue eyes and blond hair, just like their Viking ancestors.

Some of the earliest tribes to live in Europe were the Celts. They were also tall and warlike and had their own languages and religions. Over a thousand years ago they were pushed westward by invading Germanic tribes, but they survive today in Scotland, Ireland, Wales, Cornwall and Brittany.

Many Scandinavians have fair hair and blue eyes.

Many invaders swept across Europe at that time, helping to form the different nations that we know today. The native peoples of England, Holland and Germany are descended from Germanic tribes. The Russians, Poles, Czechs and other East Europeans are descended from the Slavs who came from Asia. The French, Italians and Spanish speak languages which are derived from **Latin.**

Europe is an area rich in farmland and minerals, such as coal and iron. This has made it one of the wealthiest places in the world, with many large cities and industrial regions.

In 1620, a shipload of English settlers landed on

A high percentage of Europeans work in industry.

the coast of North America and started a colony. They were among the first of many Europeans who moved to the New World. The white people of the modern United States are a complicated mixture of immigrants from Britain, Italy, Germany, Poland and Scandinavia. White Europeans have also settled in South Africa, Australia and New Zealand.

The Arabs and Persians are Caucasoid peoples as well. The Arabs of Saudi Arabia and Yemen are tall and lean with aquiline noses.

Their religion is **Islam** and they may not eat meat from pigs or drink alcohol. They pray several times every day, always turning in the direction of Mecca, the city where their prophet, Mohammed, was born.

The Arab peoples have spread to North Africa. The oldest inhabitants are the Berbers, famous for their skill as horsemen. The Tuareg and Bedouin

The Tuareg people live on the edge of the Sahara.

tribes, who live as nomads on the edges of the vast Sahara desert are also descended from Arab invaders.

Farther east, in the vast subcontinent of India and Pakistan, live other Caucasoid peoples. In the mountains of the North live the fierce Pushtuns and Afghans. They spend the harsh winters on the plains, but take their flocks of sheep and goats high into the mountain pastures in summer.

Most of the Indian people, however, are of Indo-European origin. Their ancestors came over the

Roadsweepers belong to one of India's lowest castes.

Rice growers shelter from the monsoon rains.

mountains about 1000 BC. The dominant religion is **Hinduism**, which is organized into a strict **caste system**. At the top are the priests, called Brahmins. Beneath them are the warriors, the merchants and farmers, and at the very bottom are the laborers.

Seven out of ten Indians are farmers, and most work on very small holdings. Their biggest crop is rice, grown on the southern plains where the **monsoon** season brings a lot of rain.

The Yellow-skinned Peoples

The **Mongoloid** peoples make up far the largest group of peoples. Most of them originally came from the plains of Mongolia. More than two-thirds of the world's population are Mongoloids. They cover a vast area, from Siberia in the north to Java and the Pacific Islands in the south.

Mongoloids are well adapted to bitterly cold weather.

The climate throughout this area varies greatly. In the north it is bitterly cold, while in the south it is hot and steamy. The different races have adapted themselves to where they live. Their skins are yellowish to reflect the glare of the sun. Their faces are flat, and they have an extra fold of fat in their eyelids to protect them against the cold.

The tribes of northern Asia are mostly nomads, wandering over the cold, dry grasslands of Siberia and Mongolia with their horses, goats and sheep. The Mongols live in round tents, called yurts, which are made of wool. They keep their animals in corrals made of bricks to protect them from biting winds – and hungry wolves.

These Mongol people sleep in woolen tents.

The population of China is easily the biggest in the world. One person in every four in the world is Chinese. For many centuries, most of the Chinese were peasants, growing rice and other crops on small patches of land in the valleys and fertile river deltas. But since 1949, when the Republic of China was formed by the **Communists,** modern industries have

Education is very important in China today.

Japanese goods are exported all over the world.

been growing fast. Many Chinese now work in mines and factories, which produce huge quantities of steel, machinery and chemicals.

The islands of nearby Japan are densely populated and there is little room for farming. So most Japanese work in factories or offices. Japanese goods are sent all over the world.

The people of Southeast Asia have many religions, the most widespread being Hinduism, **Buddhism** and Islam. One island which has kept its own special religion is Bali. Here, the most important food is rice, which the Balinese see as a gift from the gods.

When white people first began to explore the Pacific nearly five hundred years ago, they were surprised to find that most of the islands in the ocean were already inhabited. They wondered how these islanders had got here.

The answer is that they had "hopped" from one island to the next. From Malaysia, Mongoloid tribes crossed to Sumatra. From there they sailed the short distance to Java, then on to New Guinea and the Pacific Islands. Others came westward from South America, on balsa wood rafts blown by the **trade winds**.

Today many islanders live as they have for hundreds of years. The Micronesians use wooden canoes to fish in the sea. The Samoans trap fish in

This Samoan earns his living trapping fish.

lagoons and spear them. The soil on most of the islands is poor, so few animals are kept, and the main crops are coconuts and bananas.

The longest journey, over 4,000 km (2,500 miles), took these early adventurers to New Zealand. They became known as Maoris. Today, most New Zealanders are descended from white European settlers, but there are still many Maoris. Their ancient customs and language are preserved at special Maori centers.

Rubbing noses is the traditional Maori greeting.

The Aboriginal Peoples

The first people to live in a country are called its **aborigines**. Today, there are few surviving aboriginal tribes. Most have died out, or become mixed in with the races that followed them.

The best known are the aborigines of Australia. They have been there for more than 40,000 years – far longer than the white settlers. They are able to live in the Australian **outback**, where there seems to be no food, water or shelter.

They hunt wallabies (kangaroos), emus and lizards for their meat, knocking them down with curved boomerangs. They dig grubs out of the

Aborigines live in the harsh Australian outback.

Bushmen of the Kalahari hunting with bow and arrow.

ground to eat, and suck water from "soaks" in the earth with straws.

Sad to say, these people are gradually being pushed from their ancient lands and their traditions are dying out. The same is happening to the Bushmen, the aboriginal people of southern Africa. The last of them now live in the Kalahari desert, a barren area of tall grass and scrub.

The Bushmen are nomads. They carry with them only a few skins, bows and arrows for hunting antelope, and sticks for digging. There is no running water in the Kalahari, so they dig for special tubers which can be scraped and squeezed to give out a trickle of liquid.

American Indians were the aboriginal peoples of North America. The tribes spread out over the land so there was always plenty for them to eat.

The Indians living on the Great Plains hunted buffalo with bows and arrows. Buffalo provided them with nearly everything they needed. They ate the meat, made the hide into clothes, turned the horns into cups and used the bones for tools. The Iroquois tribes of the St Lawrence river grew many crops, including potatoes and tobacco.

Blackfoot Indians hold a celebration.

The North American Indians still try to preserve their ancient customs and languages, but most of them have been lost. This has not happened in South America, where white people find the land difficult to live in. There, many ancient Indian tribes have been left in peace.

High up in the mountains of Bolivia, the air is thin, with little oxygen. The Indians who live here have developed larger lungs so that they can breathe more easily. They live in houses made of mud bricks, and keep herds of sheep, llamas and alpacas.

The tropical **rain forests** of the Amazon are very hot and steamy. They are overgrown with jungle vegetation and full of dangerous animals, snakes and insects. Yet many Indian tribes live there.

The icy wastes of the Arctic are just as difficult to live in. The Eskimos of the far north have bodies that

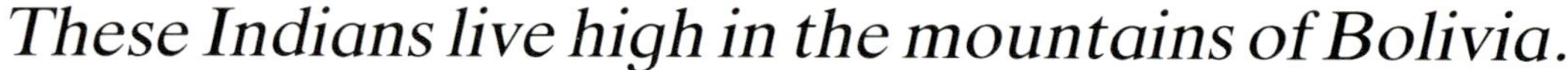

These Indians live high in the mountains of Bolivia.

Modern equipment helps Eskimos living in the Arctic.

are specially adapted to keeping heat in. Their nostrils are narrow so that little heat is lost through their noses. Today, very few Eskimos build the traditional igloos of ice-blocks, or make long hunting journeys across the ice. They have rifles and electric generators and live in modern houses.

Farther east, in the north of Norway, modern machinery has also changed the lives of the Lapps. These are nomadic people, who follow the herds of reindeer as they move about the **tundra**, and use their meat, hides and milk. Modern Lapps travel by motorized sleds, called skidoos, and keep in touch with each other by walkie-talkie radio.

Glossary

Aborigines The first known inhabitants of a country. Natives.

Buddhism A religion whose followers obey the teachings of the Buddha. It is widespread in Asia.

Caste system The Hindu division of people into four separate classes.

Caucasoids One of the major groups of races in the world, made up of people with light skins.

Communists People who believe in communism – a system of government where all industry and commerce is owned by the state.

Equator The imaginary circle that goes around the exact center of the earth at the point where the sun is overhead at midday.

Hinduism A religion, based mainly in India, which teaches the idea of reincarnation – that people have many different lives in different forms.

Ice Age A time when a large part of the earth was covered by ice.

Islam The religion of Moslems, who believe that there is only one God and that Mohammed is his prophet.

Latin The language of ancient Rome.

Mongoloids The races whose people have yellow skins and flat faces. They originally came from the plains of Mongolia.

Monsoon The tropical rainstorms that come to Southeast Asia during the rainy season every year.

Nomads Wandering peoples who have no fixed dwelling places.

Outback The remote bush country of Australia.

Rain forests Dense evergreen jungles where the rainfall is heavy and the temperatures are high.

Trade winds Winds that blow steadily toward the equator.

Tundra The area between the snowline and the treeline, where the soil is always frozen and little can grow.

Books to Read

Bell, Neill. *Only Human: Why We Are the Way We Are.* Boston: Little, Brown, 1983.

Browne, Rollo. *Aboriginal Family.* Minneapolis: Lerner Publications, 1985.

Towson, W.D. *Illustrated Atlas of the Modern World.* New York: Franklin Watts, 1981.

van der Post, Laurens, and Jane Taylor. *Testament to the Bushmen.* New York: Viking, 1984.

Picture Acknowledgments

The illustrations in this book were supplied by: Camerapix Hutchison Library *front cover*, 5, 6, 7, 11, 13, 16, 17, 18, 19, 23, 28; Malcolm S. Walker 8–9; Wayland Picture Library 14; ZEFA 4, 10, 12, 15, 20, 21, 22, 24, 25, 26, 27, 29.

Index